How to
Share A
Bad
Attitude

Includes Tips for the Times when Your Attitude Really Stinks

by Ben Goode

The Truth About Life™

Published by:
Apricot Press
Box 98
Nephi, Utah
84648

books@apricotpress.com
www.apricotpress.com

ISBN 1-885027-08-7

Cover Design & Layout by David Mecham
Printed in the United States of America

"Since you are reading this book, you probably are not swimming for your life while being pursued by hungry sharks or trapped inside a whale at the bottom of the sea."

Why worry?

Either you are well, or you are sick.

If you are well, you have nothing to worry about...except global warming, the new strains of super penicillin-resistant bacteria, gang violence, and how you're going to pay for your kids' education.

If you are sick, you have only 2 things to worry about: Either you will get well so you can keep worrying about the fat content in your hoagie sandwich, the tenderness in your glands which could be cancer, or large asteroids which could collide with the earth in this century...or you will die.,

If you die, you have only 2 things to worry about (in addition to whether your husband will finally hook up with that old girl friend from college after you're dead, who you think he likes better than you anyway, what your friends really thought of you, depletion of the Ozone layer, and the build up of chemical weapons in the third world) either you will go to heaven, in which case you have nothing to worry about...except for whether or not your neighbor, Max, is there, who bugs you...or if it's really going to be as boring as it looks...or you will go to Hell...which can't possibly be worse than all of this worrying...or... which will be a relief because everyone knows that the things you conjure up in your mind are never as bad as you think they will be...and you can finally quit worrying about going there and just enjoy it...

B.G.

Introduction

The desire to share cool stuff with other people is a part of the human DNA. So it's natural that most of us who have bad attitudes want to share those attitudes with others. Just like wanting to share any other talent: cowboy poetry, skill at the piano, the ability to dance well, creative burping, a cool new song, coughing and wheezing, your herpes flare-up, conspiratorial political philosophies, and so forth, if you have a bad attitude, naturally you want to share it. The problem is there are many people who don't know how to do this effectively.

Sharing can be a challenge, under the best of conditions, because sadly, just like with the measles, flu, leprosy, legal expenses, financial malaise, too much information, and stupidity, many people who do not have bad attitudes don't want to have certain things shared with them. Incredibly, they genuinely may not want to know about your attitude. They may be fine if you were to go through your entire life keeping your bad attitude your little secret. Even though we can punish these narrow-minded people by giving them a demeaning label such as "attitude-o-phobes," and even though you know they are entitled to your attitude whether they want it or not, you can easily see the scope of the problem.

Proceed With Caution

Λ truly bad attitude often takes years to develop; it requires a great deal of skill, combined with hard work. That's why we feel that a bad attitude is a terrible thing to waste. Yet, if done incorrectly, sharing a bad attitude can be murder. Take, for example, a friend of mine who we will call Ben because that's his name. Ben had the misfortune of being selected for an audit by the IRS. The agent we will call Erval, because we can't remember his name and because I think Erval sounds evil for a name. Anyway, the agent, who we will call Erval, found some deductions on Ben's return that he said he would not allow. Ben deferred to his accountant, who was also at the audit and who we will call Bozo, which is not his real name. Unfortunately, Bozo was having a serious bad attitude that day AND he also lacked skill in effectively conveying his bad attitude. He chose that particular moment to share his attitude with Erval by calling him an unethical creep or something to that effect. Some three years later, my friend Ben emerged from the ensuing litigation vindicated with respect to the denied deductions, but otherwise ruined from the expensive legal battles. 'Crimeny, even the clothes on his back, the gophers in his yard, and the guppies in his kids' fish tank were confiscated or levied. Bozo, on the other hand, got paid a whole bunch of money to help with said legal battles.

Another example of a person who improperly shared attitude was not a friend exactly, or even an acquaintance for that matter, but his story does serve as a good illustration of my point. His name was Achmed (pronounced A-phlegm-med) and he had some serious attitude. Achmed chose to share his attitude on Al-Jazeera TV by taunting the US Marines and Navy Seals. His physical remains are now spread throughout the Middle Eastern ecosystem as vapor and random carbon molecules, which are the foundation of life on earth, but unfortunately they will be assimilated into plant life where it is tough to continue to carry out attitude-sharing exercises against the Marines. At this point, having a camel or goat eat the plant occupied by his molecules and then expelling them at some spot where the marine is likely to step, thereby stinking up his boot, is probably the only way for Achmed to express his rage at this point.

So we see that sharing a bad attitude with others, while a useful life skill, must be done responsibly. Hopefully, after reading this book you will know better how to do this so that you can enjoy a long life of sharing your bad attitude with your friends, acquaintances, and enemies who don't necessarily want to have your attitude shared with them. It's true. This amazing book can help you effectively share your wretched attitude with others even, or especially those who really don't want to be shared with, and you can learn to do it without winding up as vapor, carbon molecules, or goat dung sooner than you might normally end up that way.

I should also point out that if you buy this book, it might also provide the author with a smidgeon of lunch money, which, if he spends it on lunch, will help provide jobs for people in the food services industry, thereby stimulating the economy. Since the rising tide lifts all boats, possibly even yours, you will become wealthier, too. So, in a way, by buying this book you will become rich(er). If I were you, I would buy one for all of my relatives and friends.

Editor's note: After publishing our last book, there were some loser-whiners who called or wrote to complain because we insulted them and then failed to insult someone else to their satisfaction. While we do our best to insult everyone, with the ever growing number of special interests, ethnic and religious groups, and whiney, pouty, sorry losers, it is becoming increasingly difficult to properly insult everyone. So, if we have overlooked your particular tender spot or special interest, we sincerely apologize. Please understand; it's not because we didn't want to insult you. We will try our best to offend as many people as we can while using, in our judgment "good taste." What more can we do?

Thank you,

B. G.

How to Share a Bad Attitude. . .

1

Using Speech to Share Your Bad Attitude with Others

One of life's great challenges is keeping ones' self from being sentenced to hard jail time for assaults arising from anger building up due to inevitable, forced contact with idiots. Idiots are the plague of our world. They are more common than bacteria in a pigpen, teenagers with cell-phones, or even weasels in congress. Yes, being surrounded by idiots can be blamed for much of the world's attitude problems. Coping with them without getting yourself arrested will be one of the great keys to your success in life. That's why sharing attitude with idiots is so important. Transferring your rotten attitude to an idiot is one thing you can do to release tension that is perfectly legal. It's not inconceivable that in some cases it could even be ethical. You can often do it by simply talking to them.

USING SARCASM EFFECTIVELY

Some very quick-witted people use sarcasm to share a bad attitude with idiots as they talk to them. These examples illustrate:

"I'm sure the reason why you didn't follow through on your conditions of probation is because the judge was talking way too fast in court last time you were there," would be a good example of an appropriate, but relatively mild sarcastic response to a deadbeat idiot making his lame excuses to the judge while he clogs up the courts with his laziness and stupidity.

"I appreciate having your goats in my yard to eat my garden and fruit trees because it reduces the fire hazard." Would be another response to a daily problem using a healthy dose of entertaining, stress-releasing sarcasm. Unless the idiot in question is completely brain-dead, it should also convey some serious attitude, possibly even starting a feud that lasts for generations.

"Maybe you should have your Mom do your homework for you to be sure it gets done next time," would be an example of an appropriate

2

response by a teacher - for example - "me", who is sick of the lame, idiotic excuses offered up by the adolescent psychotics in his High School English class. If you use this type of sarcasm, some thin-skinned students will leave your classroom in anger, if not in tears; others will be completely confused about exactly what it is that you are saying and provide hours of entertainment for you and the rest of the class.

The problem we run into all the time with sarcasm is that there are so many desperate, idiot-plagued people who have the misfortune of having been born slow-witted, dull-witted, or who have no wit at all and who struggle to come up with an entertaining sarcastic response in time to have it do any good. Therefore, we would like to share with you another very effective method of talking to idiots that will transfer your bad attitude and that also has the added benefit of helping to relieve tension.

HONESTY THERAPY

Many people are surprised to discover that frank, brutal honesty can be just as effective as sarcasm in conveying bad attitude and releasing tension when interacting with idiots, provided it is communicated without any tact. For example, let's say you return to a major university enrolled in a graduate program and one of your 50-something year-old professors shows up with a juvenile haircut, earring, and nice tattoo. He looks comical. You're embarrassed for him. By being brutally honest and completely tactless, you can totally send him spiraling upward with an attitude that may last for the entire semester by making a simple statement like, "How old are you? You dress like a goofball. I was hoping for adult professors." Each of these statements could be ABSOLUTELY HONEST, require no creativity, brain-power, or wit to speak of, and yet would almost be guaranteed to send the professor into an attitude funk that might last for weeks and months.

When I was teaching high school English years ago, I caught a student cheating red handed. When I gave him a zero on the assignment, predictably, his mom came bustling up to confront me about my unfairness. My response of, "So, you're asking me to help make a good adult citizen out of your son by rewarding him for cheating by giving him an 'A' By the way, you have strawberry jam on your lapel," was totally honest, and very effective in conveying a bad attitude that lasted for well over a decade, last I checked.

"Combing your remaining fifteen hairs up over your bald head makes you look like someone who is failing miserably as you try to fool people

4

into believing you have hair," or "You look like an over-sized laundry bag filled with billiard balls in your spandex cycling outfit," would also be examples of very true and blunt statements that would probably be very effective at conveying bad attitude.

So if you are slow-witted or no-witted, or even if you are pretty sharp, but just too tired or lazy to go to the trouble of thinking up sarcasm, you can still convey a rotten attitude effectively by simply being direct, honest and tactless.

A GREAT COMBINATION

In every walk of life, whenever you encounter idiots, if you are one who can combine sarcasm with bluntness, you can make a great contribution to humanity and I feel you have a moral obligation to do it. An approach which is only slightly less direct as "the direct approach" outlined above, but which is just as honest, can combine both sarcasm and blunt honesty. This may actually be the most effective way I know to convey a bad attitude. It will send an idiot crashing into a complete bad-attitude day every time. If you can pull it off, you should try to do it.

Let's illustrate a sample response to a standard garden-variety-type idiot who you might encounter anywhere: some goofball whose life is a wretched shambles, who can't make a relationship work, who is always broke and who blames his nice parents for his train-wreck of a life because they were, "too strict," but who continues to accept financial help from them anyway. The direct, honest approach to conveying attitude would respond something like this: "So let me understand this correctly; you yell at and otherwise abuse your wife, get fired from job after job, and had your car repossessed, all because your parents worked too hard trying to teach you to be responsible, honest, and thoughtful, and to go to church. I just wanted to make sure I understand your position."

Or another common example would be, "When I clean up these mounds of dog poop your Sparky is leaving on my lawn, did you want me to leave them on your sidewalk so guests to your house can spread them out and allow them to decompose faster, or should I stuff them into your mailbox so they will be out of sight?"

Another effective example could be, "Let me understand, you were embarrassed because you irresponsibly allowed yourself to become pregnant, and now you're worried about the inconvenience and damage to your slim figure, and so to make things right, instead of having the baby adopted by a loving couple you're going to have her killed."

6

Try this: "Did you want me to save these shells the chef left in my omlet so he can take them home to his cats?"

Or, "It was that man's fault you're in jail. I can clearly see that you had no choice other than to beat him up because he called the police when you stole the neighbor's car to go sell drugs to 12-year-olds."

SUMMARY

If you can only manage a little sarcasm, you can convey amazing amounts of bad attitude, and as a simple alternative you can fulfill your obligation to convey your bad attitude to others using the simple tool of blunt honesty, thereby doing a great service to humanity. If you have the intelligence and the energy, you can do both.

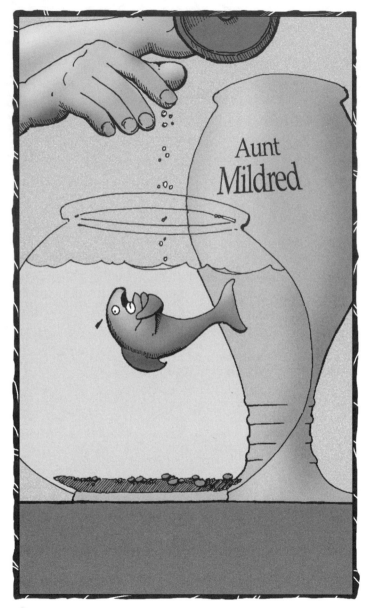

2 Using Names to Share Your Bad Attitude

One of the most common ways to convey attitude is through the use of names. Pushing someone's buttons by calling them an insulting name goes back at least to the sixties with Wally calling is little brother "Beaver," the Lone Ranger calling his side-kick "Tonto," and with one of the big, mean neighbor kids calling me something insulting that I don't want millions of readers to pick up on. Sadly, however, some of the most irritating idiots in your life are too dense to realize they are being slandered or insulted, call them what you may. That's why one of the best ways to convey bad attitude is by naming yourself. The most common subset of humans who does this with great frequency is the set of musical artists.

Besides being one of the main purveyors of misery (blues), rage (punk rock), and mononucleosis (love songs), music can also convey a whole lot of bad attitude (rap and hip hop). A few generations ago it didn't take much to shock people and convey attitude. The band known as "Beethoven" sounds like pretty tame stuff to those of us today who are conditioned to more angry music, but back in the 18th century Ludvig Van was really in your face. He proved that musicians can really convey bad attitude effectively. Then if you take legendary bands like Twisted Sister, Anthrax, Mega Death, Bad Company, Motley Crue, and Anthrax who all gave themselves these comical sounding names in order to convey bad attitude to thirteen-year-olds, you begin to see the potential. The fact that silly teen exploitation bands provide comic relief for people over 30 is beside the point. If a band wanted to convey bad attitude to people over 30 they would have to use other names like "Long Weekend, Alimony, Colonoscopy, or Kidney Stones." The fact that there aren't many bands naming themselves attitude names to convey attitude to over 30-year-olds is probably because this demographic gets plenty of attitude from their 13 to 18-year old kids, so they prefer bands with names like, "Barry Manilow" or "John Denver."

Not a lot of attitude there. So we see that it's tough to really convey a bunch of bad attitude without having a really bad attitude name. Since we know that many of our readers will struggle to come up with creative attitude-conveying names, we have thought up a few of them to help you along.

The following is a bunch of names for you to consider if you want to start a band in order to convey your contempt or bad attitude. We have done our best to conform to the cool idea of unconventional spellings used by such music icons as the BEATles, LED Zeplin, and Limp Bizkit so that you can have the necessary level of smugness to convey contempt even if you have no talent.

KOLLATERAL DAMAGE
EAR FEAR
HOWIERD STEARN
WRECK-TAL ITCH
FOOT FUN GUS
BILL MA-UR
STOOL SAMPUL
SCHTOMACH KONTENTS
DIK CHAINEY
HABEUS KORPUS
HEMUHTOMA
THE WIGGLES
PHLATULENCE
LOWBOTOMY

AAL GORE,
KOLON KANSER
ARIANUH HUFFINGTON
TOXIC WAIST
BLACK WATER

We haven't checked the copyright, so some of these names could conceivably already be used. There is one other point that needs to be made here since some of you may want to go beyond the name of your band and actually try to use your music to convey your attitude or to exploit 13-year-olds or older adults who lack higher thinking skills. I should probably illustrate how this is done.

AN ILLUSTRATION OF HOW THIS IS DONE

In 1963 a basement band, who had very meager musical talent, was practicing hard to become rock stars. Day after day, week after week, they practiced shrieking and yelling off key until finally the neighbors had had enough. They called the police. In the confrontation that followed in front of their garage, a neighbor lady called them impudent snots. Because this band's music and attitude caused this lady to become really upset and, because she was known to have cats, losing her cool and calling them impudent snots caused the band's popularity among 12-15-year-olds in the neighborhood to skyrocket. Kids came from miles around to see and hear this band, who now had the reputation of serious attitude and who had defied police. (Actually, they didn't exactly defy police. The police made them quit practicing, which for some would have been a disaster effectively ending their musical career, but for this particular band lack of practice had no impact whatever on the quality of their music.) The name stuck; although because of the kids' limited vocabulary and since their ears were ringing, they thought the lady called them impotent shots, and so that's the name that they actually gave themselves, and of course they had to change the spelling.

The group went on to have a string of tasteless hits and eventually change their name to the Rolling Stones, which brought them even more fame and popularity, proving to millions of adolescents that it doesn't take talent to make it big in the music-drug scene, just attitude. So if your vision for your future is to be arthritic and still embarrassing yourself as you hop around on stage at sixty something, but you have been told you have absolutely no musical talent, don't let that stand in your way. Go to work on your attitude. This takes very little skill and effort. And, using names can be a very effective way to share your bad attitude with others, usually without having harm done to you.

How to Share a Bad Attitude. . .

3

Sharing a Bad
Attitude Through
Fashion

The great philosopher, Ben Goode, once
observed that nearly everyone goes through life
wearing a uniform. He goes on to explain that the
purpose of this uniform is to advertise to the world
what kind of people this person wishes to have
come around and what kind he/she doesn't want to
come near. For example, if you wear a traditional
cowboy outfit with boots, wranglers and a belt
buckle in any high school in the Western U.S., you
won't have to worry too much about the Goths,
Jocks, preppies, vampires or skaters crossing the
hall to chat with you. They may pass close by to
brandish weapons or to flash their I-pods, but you
won't have to worry about figuring out what kind
of conversation would interest them. The reverse

is also true of preppies, vampires, jocks, etc...the jocks most likely won't stop to chat with you if you wear your preppie, vampire, or druggie uniform. From these examples, we can see that your uniform sends a message that is powerful enough to control many cubic yards of air and space around your person. So if you want to send a message of bad attitude, a simple, hassell-free way is to do it with your clothes and appearance.

I should also mention that clothes-attitudes can have a downside too, which can be unfortunate at times, since your uniform can act as a fence and limit the places where you can go without being assaulted. And if you happen to be a new kid who just moved into a new area with which you are unfamiliar, you will need to be careful, because you could get yourself killed wearing the wrong uniform. That's why we recommend that if you find yourself in an unfamiliar area you can keep the locals off balance by wearing something neutral like a duck costume, McDonalds uniform, or pajamas. Dress neutral for a few days giving yourself time to figure out what uniform you want to wear to keep from being beat up all the time.

Trendy fashion will change. Nothing is more certain. Only a few short centuries ago in Western Europe, guys wore tights and women wore gunnysacks, shortly thereafter fashion required three-cornered hats and huge dress rings. And fashion changes very quickly. Between the time when I am writing this book and before it goes to print, whatever fashion is effectively showing contempt and attitude will most likely already be in the process of being appropriated by older un-cool dweebes who are trying to be trendy, but who are only now finally starting to pick up on fashion that was avante guarde months or even years ago. The more trend-savvy attitude purveyors will have already moved on. So there is no point in taking time and ink here to describe specific attitude fashion; therefore, we will focus on a few basic bad attitude-conveying principles as it applies to clothing.

PRINCIPLE #1: If you plan to use your appearance to share your rotten attitude, you will want to become adept at the shock method or "JHSET" system as it is sometimes called. What this means is you should pause for a moment and ponder what you could wear to shock your Junior High School English Teacher (JHSET). If you want to convey bad attitude, that should be your standard. If you think your former teacher would be shocked if you grow your hair out 6-feet long and light it on fire, try that. If you think she would be shocked if your skirt were so small that all your glands are exposed to the first-graders, try that. If you think she would be shocked if you came to school with a camshaft drilled through your head, try that. If your JHSET sees your uniform and develops an attitude like a constipated badger, you can smirk with a vengeance, because it's probable that many other teachers and adults, possibly even including your parents will also start stomping and snorting like menopausal rhinos. And so your rotten attitude will go on down the line. For generations this method has worked because so many parents care what the Junior High School English Teacher and her peers think. If the day ever comes that people stop caring what she thinks, we will have to come up with another method of purveying attitude. But for now, this is highly effective.

PRINCIPLE # 2   Slouch. There is just something about slouching that conveys a bad attitude.

PRINCIPLE #3   Smirk. There is also something about smirking that conveys a bad attitude.

PRINCIPLE #4   Swear. There is nothing like foul language to convey contempt and attitude. And the good part is that it requires virtually no effort or intelligence at all. Observe your neighbor's Rotweiler named Sith who has been chained up to the fence between your yard for two years. In dog language he let's fly a constant stream of cuss words that are at least as foul-sounding and intimidating and angry as anything you could come up with. The dog's language of attitude affects everyone in the neighborhood: "Woof, Growl, Woof, Growl, Woof, Growl." The good news is that when you let go streams of cuss words it takes absolutely no more brain power than Sith's Bark and Growl. You can accomplish the same thing.

Hopefully, by applying these principles, particularly when used along with speech-attitude conveyance methods and name-calling attitude sharing techniques, you can become the complete attitude-sharing package and effectively share your rotten attitude with thousands, if not millions of unsuspecting people. Enjoy!

Note to people over 30. You most likely don't get it, attitude fashion that is. You may have to choose another strategy for conveying your bad attitude instead of using your uniform. If you try to intuit what would shock stuffy people you will most likely just convey the message, "Look at me. I'm an idiot."

How to Share a Bad Attitude. . .

4

How to fix a screwed up life

It seems like Sir Winston Churchill, Don Knotts, or somebody once said, "For every person digging at the root of a problem there are 100 hacking at the leaves."

I, frankly, can't see the point. Problems have absolutely nothing to do with vegetables, unless, of course, politicians get hold of them, then there's green stuff hanging all over everything along with plenty of fertilizer which usually just serves to make the problems grow bigger. No, rather than going to work on the greenery, I plan to start by solving the actual problems them-selves...starting with the problem of your misery, unhappiness, despair, neurosis, psychosis, schizophrenia, or mad cow disease.

Fact: Most unhappiness is caused by people doing stupid things. So let's go to work and solve the problems of the stupid things that YOU do. I will do this by first outlining some of your problems and then offering solutions which might work. The following are a few examples of this problem solving technique:

Problem #1: Hitting the wall with your head.
Solution #1: This is stupid. Stop doing this.

Problem #2: Stupidity.
Solution #2: This is a very big problem. If you are stupid and annoy people, they will generally do mean things to you, which could make you unhappy. Buy the book, "How to Cope When You Are Surrounded By Idiots...Or If You Are One", By Scholar, Social Scientist, and world-renowned author, Ben Goode, wherein are the answers to your problem of stupidity. If you do this, it will also help me solve...

Problem #3: Poverty, not having enough money.
Solution #3: The problem of money is normally one of perspective; Either you don't have as much as the people around you or the people around you have too much when compared with you. You must decide which and take the appropriate action. For example, if you don't have enough money relative to those around you, you can solve this problem

if you move to a place where people are poorer. If you live in Beverly Hills and feel poor, if you were to move to say, Rock Springs, Wyoming, you might just fit in perfectly after you picked up some boots and Wranglers. If, on the other hand you already live in Rock Springs and you feel poor compared to those around you, you might have to move someplace really radical like Pakistan or Bangladesh. This change of perspective should make you feel terrific.

Problem #4: Stapling your lips to your forehead.
Solution #4: This is stupid. Stop doing it.

Problem #5: You are annoying and unpopular.
Solution #5: Being annoying and unpopular can really put a damper on life. Some people, like your mom, will tell you "Just be yourself," and stuff like that. However, if you are annoying and unpopular, "yourself" is the last thing you should be since nobody already likes you and everyone treats you like dirt. No, you need a complete make-over to forcefully compel people to like you.

Change everything. If you have long hair, cut it short. If you are skinny, become plump. If you are quiet and shy, start being a pushy loudmouth.

Try this for a while, and if you still don't have enough friends, you might have to resort to the tried and true method of buying some. (If you don't have enough money to buy friends in the place where you live, you may have to down-grade your place of residence as described above.)

Problem #6: Stubbing your toe on the bed post in the night while you're going to the bathroom.
Solution #6: Use duct tape to fasten stuffed animals or chickens to all of the low hard stuff where you might stub your toe in the middle of the night.

Problem #7: You are a total screw up.
Solution #6: Read the next chapter. ◆◆

Ben Goode

5

When you are a screw up

When it comes to working with the screw ups of life, now days it is very important to assess blame. If this mess you call your life is somebody else's fault, you need to know about it so your lawyers can determine the amount of damages to claim.

Herein often lies the problem: Many bum-bling incompetents are bumbling around in complete ignorance of their own incompetence. If they had any idea what colossal screw ups they were, some of them would stop.

In view of this, here is our contribution to science and therapy, some clues which should help you determine if you are a screw up.

You are probably a screw-up if:

When you were little, whenever people would come to visit your family, your parents would hide you in the trunk of the car or in the refrigerator.

You find yourself late for work for the third time this week because you had to rummage around to find something to put over your head after you inadvertently grabbed the blow torch instead of the hair dryer again.

You lost your license to practice body piercing because your first 200 customers all died from loss of blood.

While you are sure that you don't have an eating disorder, you keep getting thrown out of restaurants because you're so enthusiastic about your new weight loss program that you can't wait until you get to the bathroom to put your finger down your throat...so you throw up all over the salad bar.

You inadvertently placed the bank bag full of money into the trash receptacle at Bacon Queen Restaurant and deposited your left over chicken nuggets in the over night bank teller.

Before you lost your license to practice thoracic surgery, on many occasions, after sewing up the patient's body cavity, his hospital 'jammies stuck out a long ways in front and you realized that it was the antenna from your TV or some other appliance from the hospital break room which you inadvertently left inside...and you repeatedly spot-welded your patients' butt-cheeks together.

At work, your associates will let you near only one computer: a 1979 IBM Pteranadon II with 2.5 bytes of RAM and 5 bytes of memory on a 5 inch floppy, because it seems that every time the whole company computer network goes down dumping everything in the system, you happen to be the one standing next to the guilty computer terminal with a stupid look on your face. And, defying all known laws of physics, you alone have proven capable of erasing all company back up files...even while fishing from a neighboring state.

Because of hundreds of little accidents over the years, you now are left with only one finger on each hand. Your family thinks this might be a sign from heaven that you're number one.

This week your boss, the chef, has made you start keeping track of what happens to the plates you drop. You are proud because you discovered that of the 33 plates you dropped this past week, 11 went directly onto the floor, 5 you caught with your foot and while the food spilled, at least you were able to keep the plates from breaking. Only 18 went into the laps of your customers.

The last time you bought a $1.79 part which you were going to personally install to fix your toilet, 2 days later you wound up calling a plumber at $50.00 an hour, a carpenter and an electrician at $60.00 an hour each and a ground crew from N.A.S.A. to unscramble the mess and get your neighbors televisions and dishwashers working again before they start a class action law suit.

After 4 years as a fishing tour guide, you celebrated having your first customer catch an actual fish...even though it weighed only 2 ounces and even though it flung itself into the boat while going after a mosquito.

It's now November. You left on your first cross-country trip driving a truck for a national company last July and today, after spending these four months driving around from state to state hopelessly lost and in 2nd gear (the only one you can find) today you finally delivered that load of tomatoes to the wrong grocery store.

Although you passed your written law enforcement tests with flying colors, you suspect that you are nonetheless in trouble because you have just finished accidentally shooting your fifth person this week for a parking violation.

After all of your bad experiences, you now refuse to accept a blind date without having your lawyer listen in on the conversation and then having your prospective date sign a 200 page pre-datual agreement.

While you don't consider yourself an alcoholic or drug addict, your family is leaving you because you are drunk or loaded most mornings by 8:00 a.m. even though you no longer have to get up that early to go to work because you can't hold a job.

No one has seen your hod carrier for 2 days. And all that you can figure is that you must have bricked him into that wall you just finished.

As a veterinarian, you get regular calls complaining that the cats you were supposed to have neutered are still capable of reproduction, but they have to drink their milk through a straw, and have voices that sound like Louis Armstrong.

The Test

These are the kinds of clues that you look for to determine if you are a screw up. However, for some of you, we need to be a little less subtle, (subtleties confuse you) so we have come up with this test. So, if you're still not sure whether or not you are a screw up, try this:

1. Your car breaks down 120 miles from nowhere. Do you:

A. Use paper clips, bubble gum, and sunflower seed shells from the floor of your car to improvise a by-pass of the carburetor and solve the problem, getting you quickly on your way again.

B. Lock your doors and wait for a highway patrolman to drive by and ignore you.

C. Lie in the road screaming in agony because you forgot to take the car out of gear and, as you were getting out, it rolled over your feet crunching all of your metacarpal bones as it accelerated off a 1000 foot cliff nearby.

2. You sit down to take a test which will determine your future income possibilities. You:

A. Take a deep breath and relax looking forward to this opportunity to "show off" what you know because of your diligent hard work.

B. Carefully get your cheat sheet out of your false arm cast and position yourself where you can get a good look at your neighbors' answer sheet so you can check your answers.

C. After a brief chat with some of the other applicants, you get out a coin to flip and a flask of emergency whiskey from your purse because you realize you devoted 6 months of your life to the study of the wrong material.

3. Your septic tank has backed up. Do you:

A. Do nothing because you don't have a septic tank.

B. Put on your hip waders, rubber gloves, gas mask, get your tools and fix it.

C. You wade in with every tool you own only to emerge 3 weeks later naked, with your hair burned off, and acid burns over 90% of your body and all of your tools and olfactory facilities irretrievably lost in the mess which, thanks to your efforts will have to be completely replaced.

If you answered "C" to any of these, unless you are on some kind of heavy medication, you are most likely a screw up. ◆◆

How to Share a Bad Attitude. . .

6 Making Your Realities Your Dreams

"It's better to aim your spear at a star and hit the ground than to throw a pipe bomb at a cat and hit your uncle Melvin's Winnebago."

-Enid Thoreau

Imagine having more money than you can spend. Picture yourself on your own yacht cruising the Caribbean with beautiful people all around you, waiters catering to your every whim. Imagine being able to travel anywhere you want, to buy huge houses, castles with cash. Imagine being able to afford a new Dodge 4X4 pickup.

Now, by contrast, picture yourself dodging those bill collectors in your '78 Datsun complete with 214,000 actual miles and those trendy rust spots. Imagine working a job you detest, with people who hate you, dining on beans and franks... Hey, if you don't have to imagine this because this is your life, lighten up. Don't get all huffy! Didn't I promise you success? Read on.

"What does imagining these two contrasting lifestyles have to do with your success", you ask? Frankly, not much, but it helps to get you into a fantasy frame of mind if I'm going to get you to comprehend this next concept: "How to become a success in life."

"The secret of success."

One day while flipping channels, I inadvertantly put my thumb on the volume button instead of the channel changer which caused the volume to go up instead of changing channels. Before I could get off from the channel I was stuck on, my neighbors and I heard a very loud motivational speaker give the following dictionary definition of success:

"Success: The achievement of a goal."

Light bulbs went off all over the place in my head. Then and there my life was changed forever. I suddenly realized the truth that if a person expects to throw up after eating caviar, whenever she does throw up from eating caviar, she is a success. When a person expects to fall on his face while ice skating...and then does...he is a resounding success.

Never before or since has one idea affected me so profoundly. From that day forward I became a huge success and you can to if you can only understand and apply this concept in your life:

"You can be successful in life only if your goals and expectations are below your actual achievements."

What this means is that if you are currently a miserable failure, all you have to do to become one of the world's great success stories is to work to get your expectations lower than your actual life. If you are able to achieve those lowered goals and expectations, by the dictionary definition, you are a success. Isn't that amazing?!? Don't you love it? You can do this!

For an example, let's say you and your spouse live in a tumbled down trailer (rented) and take in $1200.00 a month between you. If your goal has been to move into your own home in a nice suburban neighborhood, on that income you're just setting yourself up for failure and dis-appointment. If, instead, your goal was to move into a garbage can and earn $30.00 a month redeeming the bottles you pick up along road sides, right now you would have to be considered one of the great success stories in the world.

Some of you out there might have some reservations using this tactic. Stop it right now! Hey, don't feel guilty. After all, the U.S. government has approved this method. They do it all the time. When not enough applicants can qualify for elite military and fire fighting groups, they simply lower the standards, thereby raising the self-esteem of all of those people who would have had to go find jobs for which they are more suited. When too many kids who haven't applied themselves in high school can't pass the exams to get into college, they simply dumb down the exams. With so many kids failing school right now, there is a big movement afoot to eliminate grading standards altogether! If we can just get those expectations low enough, some day every child in America will be a resounding success.

One of the ultimate examples of this concept which you are all familiar with is how we've lowered standards for the president of the United States to the point that even if you have made a few mistakes, like...say...you smoked pot, or you dodged the draft, or, while, of course you are a philanderer, you messed up and weren't terribly discreet a couple of times, and you cheated on your taxes, or maybe you are a pathological liar without any shame at all or without so much as one shred of common decency. Hey, No problem. Now days even you can still be elected! Go for it!

Now, with an understanding of this important concept, go be the biggest success in the world. Make your realities your dreams. ◆◆

How to Share a Bad Attitude. . .

7 Reasons why you should be happy even though your life is a complete disaster

So you're down. We need to cheer you up. No matter what your circumstances, if a 900 pound squid has removed your mask and snorkel and is clinging to your face, if your two year old daughter has hold of your nose hairs and is flipping you around, even if the company you work for has just announced that they are laying you off and on the way out of his office, the boss gave you a noogie with a cheese grater...and then squirted you with analgesic...you can still keep a stiff upper lip, a chipper attitude even without strong medication. Consider:

❑ Your lips and ears haven't been stretched behind your head and spot-welded together.

❏ You probably didn't realize just at this moment as you are falling through the air that you forgot to connect the bunji chord to your leg.

❏ Your insides aren't on the outside of you.

❏ Even though you are so ugly you can't coax a dog to come close enough for you to pet it with a steak in your hand, your ugliness frees you to do things that attractive people can only dream of... like wearing a full-body tattoo, trying new kinds of acne medicine you found in the high school shop, and pressing your face against the window to scare people at fancy restaurants.

❏ Cat owners don't control congress.

❏ It's still legal in this country to buy a balloon, inhale the helium, and talk like a Munchkin.

❏ You're not a mackerel attached to a pop gear trolling for marlin.

❏ Since you are reading this book, you probably are not swimming for your life while being pursued by hungry sharks or trapped inside a whale at the bottom of the sea.

❏ You are not a turnip.

❏ Although you are so poor they just

repossessed your wheelbarrow and starving kids and condemned your cardboard shack so they can try to eradicate the vermin in town, you have a very low tax rate.

❏ Even if your daughter was blonde, she probably didn't date O.J.

❏ Although you belong to a family of drug-crazed, violent, part alien, cross-dressing, hermaphroditic lunatics, there is no law that requires you to go on Oprah and humiliate yourself by bearing your soul.

❏ Your head hasn't fallen off.

❏ Although you totaled your car, it was no big deal because it was only worth $600.00. Other people you know have cars worth $900.00 or even $1,000.00. In fact, the guy who you ran into must be much more unhappy than you because his car was worth upwards of $1,200.00!

❏ You don't melt when snotty little kids throw water on you.

❏ There is currently no law forcing you to eat caviar, anchovies, sushi, oysters, rocks, or gravel.
❏ Your intestinal parasites don't have conversations with you.

❏ You chuckle to yourself because although your wife has kicked you out because you're a bum and your lawyer says that you will now have to pay her two thirds of your crummy $1600.00 per month salary for alimony and child support, what she doesn't know is that you have just been diagnosed terminal from a rare disease. She will only be able to collect 2 or 3 months worth before you croak.

❏ Although you've been audited by the IRS and so now they're taking your house, boat, car, groceries and spleen and levying your pay check for the next 170 years, you had a $1.25 profit from the sale of your Upper Deck John Crotty rookie card and since there is no way they can trace the transaction, you're not going to tell them...plus your house has fleas in the rug...and your spleen has a tumor.

❏ You probably don't live inside a zit.

❏ Even if you lack the fundamental intelligence necessary to wallow successfully in a wet corral, you can still vote, watch network TV, have children and work for the government.

❏ A cow is not sitting on your head.

❏ You are not yet calcified or petrified.

❏ Even though you're broken hearted

because, after 9 years you finally gave up waiting and broke up with your boyfriend because he's unable to make a commitment. It works out for the best because later on you realize how lucky you are because you read in a tabloid that he's really a cross-dressing woman with a deep voice who is a bigamist and who makes her living fleecing other women...and all he/she got from you was your Hundai Excell.

❏ Your face isn't being used as a sledge.

❏ Most dentists don't use chain saws.

❏ Even though your politicians have nothing but contempt for you and are convinced that you are a mush-headed sap who can be manipulated at their every whim by well produced media ads, and because they can threaten to use their influence to do you harm, they will most likely never have you hunted down and killed because they like having your tax dollars to spend whenever they want.

❏ Your colon isn't connected directly to your nose.

❏ Bacteria don't grow to be as big as cows.

❏ Alien worm-like creatures aren't dangling from your nostrils. ◆◆

45

8

Failing with humans? Maybe animals will make you happy

If you're a total failure with people, some experts in the psychotic professions suggest that you get a pet for companionship instead of setting yourself up for more failure by continuing to insist on dealing with human beings. If this is the direction that you decide to go, there are some things you should know about those pets...cats especially. Very soon, on the outside of all cats, the government will require one of the following warnings to be posted:

WARNING: The main cause of the plagues of the 1300s, which wiped out over half of the population of medieval Europe, was the proliferation of black rats who were host to the fleas which carried the disease. This explosion of rats was made possible when people who believed that cats were possessed by demons did everything in their power to wipe them out. An absence of their main predatory opposition allowed the rats' population to explode. So, from the logic of Washington DC., because cats are possessed, they were responsible for the plagues of the middle ages.

Additional useful information about your pets which you should consider before using them for therapy:

❏ Because of their unique ability to mate with themselves or to grow into two complete animals when chopped in half, about the only way that I have found to successfully spay or neuter an earthworm is to drop it into a blender.

❏ Buck Hyde of Bearskid, Montana once caught a 3 pound brook trout using only the nose ring of an adolescent (which he had accidentally hooked during his back swing while casting his rod) for bait. Even more remarkable is the fact that he did it with only the half of his fishing pole that was left after it was broken over his head and with most of the line wrapped around his neck.

❏ Gladys Pipp of Knights End, Wisconsin fed her pet Boa, George, a steady diet of fluoridated baby birds for 15 years. After he died, Gladys discovered that he still had all of his original teeth, as far as she could tell.

❏ We're wondering: if you put one of those fish with the transparent skin...You know the kind you can see right into...If you put one of those in an X-ray machine, would it make it so you COULDN'T see it's bones?

❏ Bats, when dipped in batter and deep fried, still taste pretty bad.

❏ A pet store's special promotion offering a free manicure for your pet lizard with purchase of over $500 was not a big financial success.

❏ While few pets would choke to death on a spaghetti noodle, many would die from swallowing a common household cheese grater.

❏ Another way to get your neighbor's pet guppies to swim upside down is to feed them lots of Jell-O.

❏ Danny Kidd, age 6, once played with a common 4 inch night crawler from the bait box until it is estimated by his uncle Ralph, that just before it snapped, it had reached a length of over 3 feet.

❏ Most common house cats will eat their weight in mice each week, provided that mice are available and that the cat is not too well fed. On the other hand, it will take nearly a month for one mouse to eat the equivalent of one cat...and you will probably have to put it in a blender.

❏ Not only do they sing continually, keeping unwanted friends and relatives away, but parakeets make wonderful bottle corks.

❏ Vietnamese, pot-bellied pigs often get so fat that their bellies will drag on the ground. If you lead yours over one of those tire-ripper things that they have at stadium parking lots, be sure you are going the right direction.

❏ Because their life span is so short, (roughly 2 days), fruit flies rarely suffer from the degenerative diseases that so plague mankind.

❏ Determined to pre-shrink the wool of the garments he produced like the cotton ones of his competitors, Henry Grizwold of Suffolk, New Hampshire boiled his 75 sheep until they became sheep soup. And the clothes still shrunk.

❏ While, for the first 300 years of our country's existence, and even today in some cultures, dog meat has been a favorite delicacy...I'm not aware of anyone who ever got hungry enough to eat a cat. ◆◆

9

Relieve Yourself of Your Peeves

Since we ran an article some time ago asking for readers to send in their pet peeves, we have been overwhelmed. Now everybody in the world must be whining to us.

Reading all of this whiney mail is really beginning to depress me and to get on my nerves. I guess it must be therapeutic to get stuff that's bothering you off your chest and so, since misery loves company, I figured, "Why not discharge my moral obligation and print a completely random sampling of these pet peeves so others can enjoy them too?" (Note: We have used their real names when legible. If you know any of these whiners, feel free to call them up and tell them to quit sending me their whining.) To that end, I offer:

53

More of my reader's pet peeves:

Misty Knight from Denver, Colorado, says that she gets angry every time someone yanks on the chain connected to the ring in her eyebrow, nose, or lip.

Bud Ligero from Phoenix, Arizona, hates it when a check made out to "Guido," that was intended to pay for illicit drugs, bounces.

Twila Spleen from Reesty Mulch, Oregon, hates it when coming out of a public rest room, her mini skirt gets tucked into her underwear in the back...especially when no one has the guts to tell her for two days.

Rex L. Ives from Bear Digit, Montana, gets upset every time he's making a big speech in public and his teeth fall out.

Ima Sapp, from Portland, Oregon, hates having all four wheels of his car jacked up, and then, after he's crawled underneath to change the oil, having one of his kids come and kick the supports out from under it.

54

Ashlee Hutchens, my daughter's friend from just outside Hooper, Utah, thinks it stinks when she gets in @#*>! trouble for @#*>! cussing even though her @#*>! teachers cuss at her first.

Elleno Decaca from Animal City, Wisconsin, gets peeved whenever she's really car sick and someone opens a can of dog food right under her nose.

Rusty Clave from Septic Falls, Idaho, hates it whenever he asks a girl to dance and she runs screaming to call the police.

Madge from Bear Skid, Wyoming, gets really worked up whenever her husband, Scooter, gets the remote during football season.

Wesley Schmurtz from Amoebae Springs, South Dakota, hates it when aliens abduct people and then eat them just to satisfy their curiosity about how humans taste.

Sal Peter, from Philadelphia, Pennsylvania, gets upset whenever he and his buddies do a drive by shooting and then when they go by one more time every-body throws him out of the car.

Bart Hemlock from Farmington, New Mexico, gets torqued at being dragged face down in the dirt behind his Jeep and having his nose fill up with rocks.

Patty Delfeo from Virginia City, New Mexico, hates it when her date puts a bag over her head and then forgets to take it off when he drops her off back at home.

Stu Carne hated it when he was feeding the last of the fish food from the urn on the window sill to his guppies and realized too late that those flakes were, in fact, the last remains of his Aunt Mildred.

Thorette Sharpe from Permawedge, Colorado, gets really upset when her new medication kicks in and she suddenly realizes that the person she was saying vicious things about is also the person she has been saying them to.

Felix Del Gato of Medicine Ditch, Washington, says he hates it whenever he's robbing a 7-11 store and his ski mask twists so that he can't see out the eye holes and so he walks into the closed doors as he's trying to escape.

Melvin Delgordo from Puckerbrush, Nevada, hates bunji jumping off a 1000 foot high bridge and realizing on the way down that he only connected the chord to the elastic on his Jockey shorts.

Dan Carafea of Verminberg, Arkansas, gets disgusted every time he has a hot date with a girl who loves cats, and then finds he has nothing to clean the fur and cat parts out of his grill, except for dental floss.

Ann Nesia from Roach Clip, Colorado, hates it when she falls asleep in class and her drool fills up her shoes.

Sandy Bottoms of Dumpling, South Dakota, gets really worked up when she wipes out while water-skiing with jogging weights on her feet and the boat forgets to come back and pick her up. ◆◆

How to Share a Bad Attitude. . .

10

An anger management technique from the annals of history

In a smoky card room in an isolated backwater town in Colorado toward the end of the 19th century, old Jake is finally winning at poker... apparently too much. The steely eyed stranger, after losing his fifth straight hand, accuses him of cheating. The cards fly. Patrons dive for cover as both men back cautiously onto the dance floor. Feeling a sudden rush of adrenaline-induced courage, Jake calls the stranger a scrawny, bug-eyed, gap toothed, rattler-polecat with poor personal hygiene.

Jake draws, but not fast enough. Before he can complete the motion, he is hit in the face by a blast which knocks him backward into a puddle of Pepsi spilled there by one of the now cowering bar patrons.

That quickly, in a split second, it's over. Clint, Jake, and Stanley stare in disbelief at the little plastic cowboy. This is their first loss in over 30 pretend, little plastic cowboy and Indian water melon seed gunfights.

Once again, although tempers flared, although insults were hurled back and forth, and even though the stranger is indeed a bug-eyed, gap toothed, rattler-polecat with poor personal hygiene, the locals are forced to admit that he can squirt a watermelon seed quicker and straighter than the best they can put forward. Thankfully, because these men were trained in the latest anger management technique, "displaced diversion" the story has a happy ending. They all shake hands and go back to playing BINGO.

This amazing anger management strategy was developed near the end of the civil War by Dr. Enos Freud as a part of a government funded program to reduce the number of war and card playing fatalities, to help those with a genetic predisposition to cowardice, and to provide jobs for the dozens of government workers who might otherwise lose their draft deferment. According to 19th century government records, many theoretical lives of family men who still enjoyed a good brawl, but who didn't want to leave helpless widows and orphans behind were saved by this innovative program.

This pioneering effort spawned dozens of scientific social experiments, some of them quite entertaining and most expensive. Even today, progressive social scientists with big government grants and excessive time on their hands are devising programs similar to this in order to make the world a better place and insure that the amount of their department's entitlement to government funds doesn't get reduced. For example, programs have been devised to attempt to rehabilitate the youthful criminal element and give them a release for their anger other than by shooting someone or biting off a chunk of their ear. There have been programs such as midnight basketball, graffiti art, lighting cats on fire, and drive-by paint gun shootings (The weapons being similar to large cake decorators).

Some opponents to these programs ask, "Shouldn't we change strategies and make parents more responsible to raise their own kids?" and, "Where the government has to step in, maybe they could insist that the kids learn to work, and be responsible...and provide more parental, "when I was a boy or girl" lectures."

Opponents to these opponents, on the other hand, point out that many people don't want their kids to know what they were doing when they were kids, and that there isn't enough time in a modern day to expect parents to lecture kids like they used to. This is a job for school principals, and scientists receiving grants from government programs.

We think the government should give us a large grant to study "displaced diversion." ◆◆

11

Ask Dr. Angst

The following are excerpts from the mental health column written by Dr. Henry Angst which appears daily on his web site -www.Lobotomy.com

In addition to his pseudo professional duties, Dr. Angst, "Psychiatrist to the Internet", is also a veterinary gynecologist, a hang-glider tester, and works part-time as an automobile lubrication technician at "Greasy Lube."

Q: Last week my pet dachshund, Fritz, went berserk, crawled through the accordion exhaust tube connecting my dryer to the outside of the house and was subsequently run over while crossing the highway, trying to get to the neighbors' schnauzer who was in heat. His little carcass has been lying there for a week between the two white stripes getting flatter and flatter and looking less and less like a dachshund. Because he's been my only family, this has been a very traumatic experience for me. I have fallen into a depression that I can't get out of. Is there any way to replace this loyal canine love that I've lost?

--Edselene Quagmire, Slippery Pit, West Virginia

A: Dear Ms Mire, Many people find that the constant cheery chirping of a parakeet can help to bring them out of a depression and give them a new start. On the other hand, after 2 days with incessant parakeet chirping, my sister went off the deep end and ran hers through the "pots and pans" cycle on her dishwasher. So, try the parakeet and if it doesn't work for you either, try taking up a physical sport like rodeo, demolition derby or kick boxing.

Q: Years ago I experimented regularly with illicit recreational drugs. Later, both of my children were born normal, except, of course, for the gills and fins. However, I find that I am troubled by an occasional flashback. These seem to be increasing in frequency and intensity and picture brightly colored worms and grubs dancing the Macarena in

64

annoying political info-mercials. Some happen at very inopportune times, like when I'm driving my Volkswagen microbus on the freeway. What do you suggest?   --Phil Armonic, Hog Smooch, S.D.

A: While there's probably nothing you can do to stop the flashbacks, since your brain is fried already, you could at least make enough money from selling those kids to the circus or aquarium to support a new drug habit. You might as well start again, since you drive a V.W. microbus and everyone, including the cops, will hassle you because they just assume you're a warmed-over, drug-crazed hippie throwback from the '60's.

Q: My boyfriend is leaving me for another woman who is better looking. In an effort to manipulate him and make him feel sorry for me, I have attempted suicide once by cutting my wrists with a plastic spoon and a second time by overdosing on my mother's MIDOL®. This strategy doesn't seem to be working. He doesn't act anywhere near as miserable and distraught as I think he should. What would a registered pseudo professional like you recommend?   --Melissa Del Gordo, Littleton, CO.

A: Melissa, next time try punishing him with the silent treatment and loud sighs, alternating with hysterical screaming. Guys love those things.

Q: I am a compulsive liar. I am always getting caught but never seem to get into trouble. The real catch is that I absolutely love to lie. I lie for practical reasons, sport, and just for fun...about everything. (And I also like to wear women's clothing, go shop lifting with my wife, and beat the illegal aliens who clean my house, just for the heck of it.)

I wouldn't worry about my lying, but since I became President of the United States back in 1992, all of my close friends have gone to prison while lying for me and now they're starting to make me feel guilty too, because I won't do anything to get them out. This massive accumulating pile of guilt is starting to make me feel so low that I'm afraid I might commit suicide or something.

--Bill Smith (Not his real name) Washington DC.

A: Dear Mr. Smith: Okay.

Q: I am a very very very overweight, pudgy person who rarely thinks about my weight, which is excessive and embarrassing, because my clothes don't fit any more because I'm so plump. In order to get this extra excessive weight off, I do an hour of aerobic exercise 12 times a day. I also haven't eaten anything but water since August 30,1987 when I had a delicious, scrumptious glazed donut

66

with lemon filling that was to die for. But I quickly put my finger down my throat so I don't think that any of the calories made it into my actual blood stream.

How can I get this extra weight off and still keep my healthy outlook on food and my body?

-- Bea Cormorant, Fort Vegemite, Nebraska

A: My Aunt Mildred had a weight problem like yours for a few years before she died. The thing that finally got every bit of unwanted weight off her was when she started a regimen of regular Mr. Clean, walnut shell, and Spun-glass enemas. (Don't try this yourself without doctor's supervision.) Unfortunately, just when she was about to finally reach her optimum weight, she died. We buried her inside a curtain rod. ◆◆

12

Odds & Ends

My Grandma Goode always said...actually, the type of things my grandma Goode always said were: "Merrill!" (That was my grand pa) "Get the mud off your boots before you step in the house!" and "Ben!" (That was me.) "You can't be full. A growing boy like you can surely eat one more piece of pumpkin pie." (Grandma thought the reason why I was so skinny was because my mom, her daughter in law, wasn't feeding me and the only cure was a month at her house where she would sit on my chest and dump food into my mouth)... But, now that was a long time ago, and it had little to do with your crummy attitude. Besides, I think at some time, grandma might have said something like "Whenever you get tired of viewing the lead-dog's backside, you can always close your eyes and visualize a cheese burger." And she certainly would have wanted you to have a good attitude... and to clean the mud off your feet. So to that end, the attitude stuff, not the dirty feet, I have compiled these bits of wisdom and information to help you through life and to help you develop a better attitude.

❏ A way to tenderize wild game, making it almost as tender as the backside of a cyclist who just finished a cross country trip, is to put it on the sidewalk or a flat rock, then beat it vigorously with a maul or sledge for an hour... Then pick up the fibers remaining, being careful not to get cement or rock chips in the mix. Marinate these over night in Liquid Plumber. Even if it tastes kind of lousy, you'll find that whatever's left will be the most tender meat you ever ate.

❏ Season your stew with anything you want, but don't let your buddy, Stu, go into the forest during hunting season in his Rudolph costume.

❏ When your basement's already filled up with water, it's probably time to turn the guppies loose and let them have some fun.

❏ Many vegetarians, long plagued by nutritional and immune system deficiencies are finally getting some relief using a good old fashioned treatment. Researchers at Gump State institute for Sociopathic Medicine have found that they get fewer colds and have more energy when they pick up a little extra protein from the common cereal weevil usually found in their granola and Grape Nuts. Dr. Aanos Brainmold insists that since he started a daily regimen of not picking out the weevil in his Granola...combined, of course, with an hour-a-day of aerobic exercise, consistently getting his 8 + hours of uninterrupted sleep since his kids moved out, sneaking an occasional Big Mac on the side, added to his weekly gelatin, bean sprout and tofu enemas, and since they finished his chemotherapy, his energy level has tripled...and he hardly gets sick any more. 'Atta boy Doc!

❏ To cure memory loss...

If you suffer from memory loss, don't spend the big bucks for Alzheimer's treatment, electric shock, or a brain transplant, simply roll up a newspaper* and hand it to your spouse. Have him or her whack you over the head when you forget your kids' names.

If your spouse is the one with the failing memory, just reverse the process.

Let's say you told your husband that you wanted a new diamond tennis bracelet for your anniversary. A week later, you bring it up again and he doesn't even remember the conversation. Grab the rolled-up newspaper, repeat your request for the diamonds and whack him a good one. Repeat the process until memory improves.**

* If newspaper is in short supply, you can also use an umbrella, hockey stick, shovel or rake, etc...

** One caution: If the instrument is too heavy or too sharp (I.E. a sledge or maul) instead of enhancing memory, it could sometimes actually serve to impair it slightly. This can be bad. Use caution.

❏ Unless you like phlegm in your scrambled eggs, it's best to wait to complain about the food until after the meal is eaten.

❏ If you feed stray dogs, maybe you can convince them to poop on your neighbor's lawn out of respect...or then again, maybe instead, they will have babies in your garage.

❏ People who sneeze too much should avoid poking grass up their noses.

❏ The best way to make a baby stop crying long enough to take a picture is to hand them a lemon slice.

❏ As a bonus, you get entertaining pictures.

❑ Whenever you're fixing breakfast for the Pope, let him put his own tabasco on his eggs...and be sure that the biscuits and gravy haven't been in the fridge more than a couple of weeks.

❑ Unfortunately skunks rarely die with their backsides buried in the ground.

❑ If you're truly concerned with what other people think about you, then don't wear your underwear on the outside of your clothes. ◆◆

Glossary: gloss/eh/ rhee - A collection of textural glosses.

Bulimia:

That annoying thing some girls do whenever they see someone they think is really disgusting and they do a kind of sign language thing where they put their finger part-way down their throat and fake like they're going to throw up...and then laugh.

Compulsive behavior:

Stuff that's real fun but which you don't want to do too often...like putting your tongue on a battery or staying up all night to watch the Star Wars trilogy and eating pizza.

Euphoria:

The feeling of bliss and extreme happiness that actors apparently feel whenever they are being filmed in a commercial.

Ivan Pavlov

(Also known as "Ivan the Terrible"): The twisted, neurotic foreigner who spent billions of government dollars in bogus research projects. When finally they threatened to cut off his grants, he wrote this lame paper about how his drooling dogs could trick him into ringing a bell or something. Amazingly, they bought off on it and now he's famous, but also pretty much dead as far as we know.

Mad Cow Disease:

A dangerous condition where whenever afternoon TV ratings in the agricultural working section of the world dropped off, and so to teach people a lesson, Oprah, who had just squished another bathroom scale flat, declared herself a temporary vegetarian immediately influencing all the people in Western Civilization who don't want to get jobs because that would mean they would have to miss "The Show" to stop eating Big Macs which caused the beef prices to plummet which, in turn, made all the cows mad...and it didn't help the ranchers either.

Narcissism:

Similar to Exorcism, but because it's a bigger and harder word, fewer people understand it...while I understand it perfectly.

Neurosis:

A term that's useful in explaining other people's weird behavior. Whenever they really get on your nerves, you can call them neurotic. i.e.. When your son wants to play football, but your ex-wife won't sign the release, she could be called neurotic. Now that you mention it, all ex-wives are usually neurotic.

Psycho analysis:

The act of trying to understand what is going on between the ears of someone who is a neurotic, (see above) bone- headed, nitwit and then talk things through and make them comprehend what anyone else in the universe with an IQ over 2 can see is obviously going on, and to get them to do the sane, rational thing that you want them to before they screw up their lives. Very difficult to accomplish over the phone.

Shrink:

What happens to your bank account whenever you have to pay for treatment.

Sigmund Freud:

Chinese rock singer who's real name was "Pink Freud" who casted his rock videos using the "couch" method. He made jokes about guys who spend most of their time thinking about football. He was eventually accidentally destroyed when he tried to save Pavlov's dogs because they were being put to sleep when they became too old to drool any more. I think he signed the Declaration of Independence, or the Treaty of San Juan Guadeloupe or something. Truly a pioneer mental case.

Xenophobia:

A silly word which proves that spelling in the English language was invented by schizoid nut cases or foreigners...or, they could have been playing some kind of practical joke in which case my respect for them just went sky high, otherwise... take for example "Xenophobia" which is spelled "xenophobia" when, if I or any other sane, rational, American-speaking adult were making up the spelling rules around here would be spelled "feer ov zenuh." And how about all these other words which make absolutely no sense like "rhythm" or "chamois" or "paradigm", which, without my daughter's help, I can't get close enough to the correct spelling for the spell-checker on my computer to correct. ◆◆

A touching letter from one of my readers.

The following is an example of the kind of fan mail I get daily:

Dear Mr. Goode,

I am a 17 year old High School junior who feels compelled to write this letter to share with you how your books have changed my life.

Just a few short months ago I was in terrible shape. I was addicted to heroine, PCP, LSD, R.F.D., and B.F.D. I was Moll to the head gangster in the gang, the Scripts, and I'm embarrassed to admit having cheated on him for the whole time with a Teflon® salesman who was named George until we got caught and they shot him. To give you an idea what a disaster my life had become, I even slumped so low that I sold my body to get money to buy Cinamon Toast Crunch and a pair of Doc. Martins. For a while I was an Iraqi spy. I had poor personal hygiene, refused to do my home work, was an assassin, ate red meat, voted for the Clintons and was a litter bug. Few non-politicians I know had ever sunk so low.

Then it happened. I found one of your books in the dumpster I was sleeping in. I read for hours, unable to put it down. The riveting humor, the caustic social analysis, the disgusting booger humor so inspired me that I determined then and there to turn my life around.

80

Now, I am happy to report that drugs, except for regular doses of penicillin and a special shampoo for recurring head lice, are a thing of the past. You will be pleased to know that after reading your second book, I was so inspired that I started going back to school regularly and turning in my homework. I now have a 5.0 GPA and was recently elected homecoming queen and cheer leader. Just this week, I received word that I have been accepted into Harvard Medical School and I've been invited to be the first teenage astronaut.

I want you to know that if you're ever on drugs or find yourself donating to the DNC, should you ever want to get back into teaching, a position with the post office, or as President or something, please feel free to use my name as a reference.

Sincerely, you're devoted fan groupie for life,

(Name withheld)

'The Truth About Life' Humor Books